Schlemiel...Schlimazel? Mensch

An Entertaining Guide to Becoming the Best You Can Be

by
Marty Bergen
and
Thomas Spector, Ph.D

Bergen Books
9 River Chase Terrace
Palm Beach Gardens, FL 33418

Copyright 2002 © By Marty Bergen.
All rights reserved including the right of reproduction
in whole or in part in any form.
First Edition published 2002.
Printed in the United States of America.
10 9 8 7 6 5 4 3 2 1

First Printing: February, 2002

Library of Congress Control Number: 2002090627

ISBN 0-9716636-0-2

Dedication

*In Memory of
Dorothy Frankel,
My Loving Grandmother*

*Grandma,
I finally came back
to my roots.*

Acknowledgments

Layout, design, and editing by
Cynthia DeZess.

Our thanks to:
Philip Alder, Margot Bennett, Cheryl Bergen,
Florence Bergen, Eileen Brenner, Laura Brill,
Nancy Deal, Ned Downey, Sybie Ferguson, Pete
Filandro, William Foster, Jim Garnher, Terry
Gerber, Lynn and Steve Gerhard, Melissa
Gersh, Latrescia Goss, Meredith Gunter, Nancy
Hammond, Julia Hough, Steve Jones, Alan
Karpe, Doris Katz, Jim Kisco, Joseph Lane,
Larry Lerner, Patty Magnus, Grace Migdol,
Sherry and Dave Milke, Harriet and David
Morris, Jan Nathan, Phyllis Nicholson, Dan
Oakes, Mary and Richard Oshlag, Dr. Michael
Pickert, Helene and Bill Pitler, David Pollard,
Jesse Reisman, Susan and Rufus Rhoades,
Marcia Satterthwaite, Nancy Stamm, Merle
Stetser, and Susan Wallach.

To order autographed copies
of this book or any of
Marty Bergen's other books
call
1-800-386-7432
or e-mail:
mbergen@mindspring.com

For additional information
please refer to pages
282-283

PREFACE

In the beginning....

One day as I was talking with my son, Bobby, I made a suggestion about a problem that was bothering him at work.

"That's a great idea," he said. "Thanks, Dad. You've really got a lot of good advice. You should write a book."

Talk about making my day! What parent wouldn't be thrilled to hear those words from his adult child?

I found myself thinking about his suggestion. Why couldn't I write a book about what I had learned over the years? It would be nice to give people some idea of how to deal with life without having to stumble around in the dark. If only I had such a book when I was 25.

From then on, everywhere I went, I would take pen and paper to jot down ideas as they popped into my head. When I got home, I would run to the computer and type them up. Soon I was ready to begin.

I already had an idea for the format. I kept hearing, "Sorry, no time now, got to run," and "Books? Who has time for books? I'm lucky if I get a chance to glance at the paper." In this age of instant information, if people are going to pick up a book, the author had better get to the point ASAP.

I was happy to try to give people what they wanted — an easy read that wouldn't take weeks to finish. But how could I make it fun and interesting?

I struggled with the way to define a person who really had his/her act together. Someone who did the right thing, and had all of the positive qualities I was trying to encourage. I was at a loss.

Then one day, my mother told me about a neighbor who had helped her out. She was so grateful that he had taken time out of his busy day to solve her problem. "Marty, that man is a real mensch," she said.

Yesssss, that's it, my quest is over. A Yiddish word, but one quite familiar to many people living in the 21st Century. I would use "mensch" to demonstrate the right way to do things. However, pointing out what to do was not sufficient. I needed a character to illustrate what *not* to do. Where's the phone? Time to call Mom.

"What's the opposite of mensch?"

"It's 'schlemiel,' Marty," she answered. "Why do you want to know?"

"Tell you later. Love ya, got to run."

It was perfect. The two characters could show the way. Now I had all that I needed for my collection of entertaining, practical tips. Except a catchy title.

Let's see: *Everything I Wish I Knew Sooner?* No way, that's totally BORING. Is there a word that rhymes with mensch? *Mensch, Shmensch?* I don't think so. Hmm, this is a lot tougher than I thought. Then, suddenly, it dawned on me.

From my youth, I recalled the chant, "schlemiel, schlimazel, hossinpheffer incorporated." It was from the popular TV show "Laverne & Shirley," where Penny Marshall and Cindy Williams would say those words before every episode. Many people would remember that line. It definitely was catchy. Hopefully, others would agree, or at least be intrigued by the title.

I hope that you will find this book to be helpful and fun. I enjoyed writing it. I certainly hope you enjoy reading it.

Marty Bergen

CONTENTS

CONTENTS

INTRODUCTION

Many of the tips in this book came from personal experiences with a variety of people. In addition to "mensches" who demonstrated the right way to conduct oneself, we are most grateful to all of the "schlemiels" who served as models of how *not* to conduct oneself. Most tips are presented as "schlemiel-mensch pairs," others seemed more effective as "singles."

Not all of the material originated from us. "Do Right By Your Body" was contributed by professional nutritionists, our computer advice originated from computer experts, etc.

We have always believed that a smart person is one who knows how important it is to be surrounded by even smarter people. Having learned to benefit from the wisdom of others, we hope the pages that follow will give you an opportunity to do the same.

1

WORDS TO THE WISE

kvetch	to complain, whine
maven	an expert
mazel tov!	congratulations!
meshugina	crazy
oy vey	oh, NO!
schlimazel	an unlucky person
shlep	to drag along
shmendrik	a puny pipsqueak
shmo	laughable, pathetic, the butt of a joke
shtick	an act or performance
tukhis, tush	derriére
yenta	a gossip, nosy busybody

WORDS TO THE WISE

S   sad sack

C   careless

H   hapless

L   lost cause

E   egotistical

M   mean-spirited

I   immature

E   easily led astray

L   loser

M   mature

E   even-tempered

N   nice — very nice

S   sensible

C   considerate

H   honorable

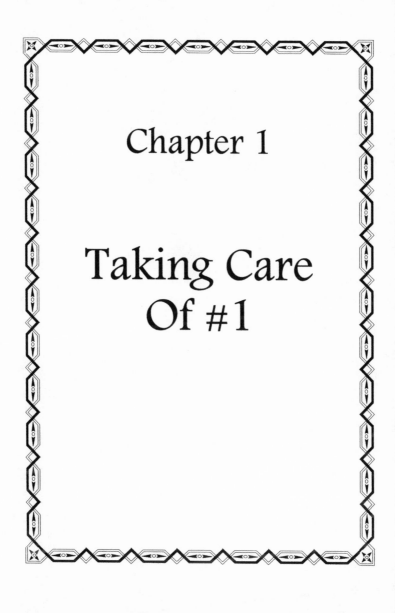

Chapter 1

Taking Care
Of #1

A Deluxe Environment

Take a moment to reflect on where you spend most of your time. Wherever this place may be, make it as comfortable as possible. Why not take care of number one?

A Schlemiel...

is eager to pass the buck when something needs to be done, even if it's very important to him. When he hates the result he screams, "You idiot! You screwed up again!"

A Mensch...

does not ask others
to do something she
can do for herself.
She knows that no one
could possibly care
about the outcome
as much as she does.

A Schlemiel...

is consumed by thoughts
of what others have
that he does not.
"My neighbor's wife looks
like Melanie Griffith,
but mine reminds me of
Andy Griffith!"

GREED IS
A TERRIBLE THING

A Mensch...
is grateful for what
she does have, knowing
that some people
have next to nothing.
For every person who has
more than you, there are
ten others who have less.

PARANOID
(AND PROUD OF IT)

A Schlemiel...

blames everyone
but himself when
he thinks about what's
wrong with his life.
"Oy vey, you're all
out to get me!"

A Mensch...

realizes that if she's
not satisfied with the way
her life is going,
it's time to look in the
mirror and remember
who's in charge.

A Schlemiel...

wakes up unexpectedly at 4:00 a.m. and wastes hours tossing and turning in a desperate attempt to get back to sleep. When this fails, he starts his day tired and cranky.

A Mensch...

gets up and finds
something to do.
The activity may tire her
out enough to go back
to sleep, but if she can't,
she is delighted to have
a head start on her day.

A Schlemiel...

is doomed to repeat the same mistakes over and over again. Unwilling to learn from the past, he continues to fail just as miserably as he did before.

A Mensch...

tries to learn from
all of her experiences,
even the negative ones.
Having learned her lesson
the first time around,
her goal is to never make
the same mistake twice.

SAVE THE BEST FOR LAST

Avoid sharing your secrets with someone until you are sure that you can trust them. A premature disclosure may come back to bite you in the tukhis.

I Can See Clearly Now

When you're wrestling
with a tough decision
and there's no end in sight,
try the following:
list all the pros and cons.
This may help you
find the light
at the end of the tunnel.

You Deserve A Treat Today

Don't wait for a special
occasion to treat yourself
to your favorite food.
Go ahead and splurge
once in awhile.
Enjoying good food is one
of life's great pleasures.

Was It Good For You?

The next time someone offers you a "great deal," stop and ask yourself, "is this great for **me**?" Too often, his idea of a spectacular deal is a lot better for him than it is for you.

Aging Gracefully

When you wake up
in the morning feeling
reasonably well and
your brain still seems
to be working okay —
it's a good day, regardless
of whether or not
the sun is shining!

HOW TO KNOW
IF YOU KNOW IT

A good way to determine if you have mastered a concept or technique is to explain it to someone. If they are able to follow along with you, chances are you know it.

THEY LAUGHED AT COLUMBUS TOO

Don't be a slave to "conventional wisdom." If your way of handling a situation does not hurt anyone and you're not breaking any laws, don't be afraid to "do your own thing."

GO AHEAD, MAKE MY DAY!

When someone criticizes
or disagrees with you,
consider the source.
If he is a real shmo,
you should be relieved and
delighted that he doesn't
see eye-to-eye with you.

LET THE BUYER BEWARE

When dealing with a new
company, be cautious.
Write down the names
of everyone you speak to,
along with all potentially
useful information.
You'll be ready in case
they try to pull a fast one.

NAME, RANK, AND SERIAL NUMBER ONLY

If you are involved in a car accident, don't give any information to the insurance adjuster for the other driver. No matter how pleasant he is, remember: he represents the other guy.

Don't Let Them
Get You Down

There are plenty of
schlemiels in the world
who will try to make
you feel inferior.
However, without your
consent, they cannot
possibly succeed.

DON'T EXPECT FIREWORKS EVERY DAY

Many people are only impressed by extraordinary events. However, if your day was "ordinary" simply because you had no major mishaps, you should be delighted, and have no regrets.

THE MEEK SHALL NOT INHERIT THE EARTH

Don't be afraid to ask
for what you want.
Going through life
wondering "what if"
is a lot worse than being
denied and moving on.

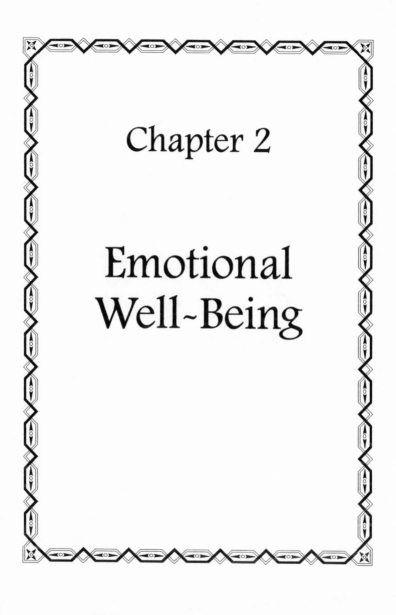

Chapter 2

Emotional Well-Being

IT ALL STARTS WITH YOU

How you see yourself is
infinitely more important
than how others see you.
If you can look back
on your day and say,
"Today, I was a mensch,"
that's really
all that counts.

BURYING HIS
HEAD IN THE SAND

A Schlemiel...

expects a bad situation
to clear up all by itself.
Too often, he neglects
the problem until it gets
so much worse that
even an Einstein
couldn't find the solution.

A Mensch...

identifies a problem,
addressing it before
it gets out of hand.
She never puts off until
tomorrow what needs
to be done today.

Bewitched, Bothered, and Bewildered

A Schlemiel...

is overwhelmed by the events of day-to-day life. He blows a gasket when things go wrong, unable to deal with the stress. "Another problem! Damn! I can't take it anymore!"

CALM, COOL, AND COLLECTED

A Mensch...

knows that sometimes life
gets a little crazy.
Instead of freaking out,
she keeps her cool
by making sure to set
aside time every day to
relax and reduce stress.

A Victim Of Circumstance

A Schlemiel...

is an eternal pessimist,
expecting the absolute
worst in every situation.
He dwells on his past
misfortunes, convinced
that he's cursed with
a miserable existence.

A Mensch...

is realistic about the
ups and downs in her life.
Instead of thinking about
what might go wrong,
she forges ahead,
eager to see what
life has in store for her.

A Schlemiel...

frets and fusses over
every little delay,
hating the inconvenience
of being forced to wait.
"My afternoon is shot —
I got nothing done while
waiting to see the doctor!"

A Mensch...
does not expect
the universe to revolve
around her schedule.
Whenever a delay is
possible, she makes sure
to bring along that book
she's been eager to read.

A Not - So - Admirable Trait

A Schlemiel...

is very sensitive about
what others say to him.
His easily-bruised ego
makes everything
a potential accusation.
"What did that mean —
did he just insult me?"

An Admirable Trait

A Mensch...

is very sensitive to **the feelings of others.** She tries to see things from their point of view, instead of looking at every situation as if only her own feelings matter.

A Glutton
For Punishment

A Schlemiel...

heads for the racetrack even though he knows he has a gambling problem. When his horse loses (again), he swears he'll never come back — which is what he said last time.

AN AVOIDANCE PLAY

A Mensch...

knows how difficult it is
to resist temptation.
She is smart enough
to steer clear of things
that get her into trouble.
By doing so, she avoids
having to "fight the urge."

THE LAST ANGRY MAN

A Schlemiel...

expresses his anger
without considering
the consequences.
That may work for him,
but it annoys the hell
out of those around him.

A Mensch...
is careful not to
fly off the handle.
When she is angry,
she excuses herself
and finds a way
to vent her frustrations
without annoying anyone.

49

A Schlemiel...
lacks the self-confidence
to accept himself
for who he is.
He gets no satisfaction
from his accomplishments,
because he knows someone
else has done it better.

DOESN'T NEED
A CLAIM TO FAME

A Mensch...

is willing to accept
herself for who she is.
She is not preoccupied
with the accomplishments
of others, knowing that
not everyone can be
a Madame Curie.

DON'T HOLD YOUR BREATH

Somewhere in the world,
your "soulmate"
or "dream home"
may well exist.
However, life is
just too short; you can
be happy without always
seeking perfection.

Enjoying A Visit
To The Dentist

The next time you are
trapped in the chair
at your dentist's office,
let your mind wander.
Recall your favorite
memory of making love.
You might even be sorry
when the drilling is over.

Accentuate
The Positive

We all have chores that we're not thrilled about. However, you can put a "positive spin" on anything. Instead of dreading the drudgery of housework, look forward to enjoying your nice, clean home.

LAUGHTER IS THE BEST MEDICINE

Don't be afraid to laugh at yourself when you do or say something silly. Even a mensch makes mistakes — and seeing the humor in them will ease the tension and make you feel better.

ALL WORK AND NO PLAY MAKES JACK A DULL BOY

From time to time, pause and reflect on what you would **like** to do, rather than what you **must** do. Thinking about something you enjoy doing is a wonderful diversion from the daily grind.

PUTTING THINGS IN PERSPECTIVE

We all have days when nothing seems to go right. However, if you think back to the horror of September 11, 2001, you will be able to cope with a fender-bender without freaking out.

Feeling Groovy

Do all of the following,
at least once a day:

1. Laugh out loud
2. Make someone happy
3. Say "I love you"
   (and mean it)
4. Give a hug, get a hug
5. Appreciate your life!

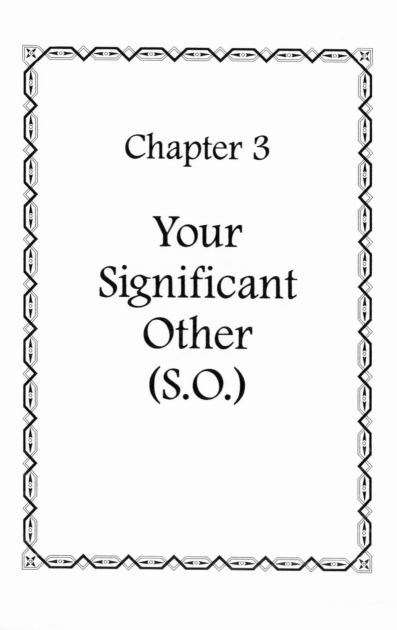

Chapter 3

Your Significant Other (S.O.)

LOOK BEFORE YOU LEAP

When a relationship
becomes serious,
step back and take stock
of the situation.
If the relationship seems
to be headed in the wrong
direction, don't rule out
premature evacuation.

STRANGE BEINGS
FROM ANOTHER PLANET

A Schlemiel...
makes no attempt
to understand why his
partner is so meshugina,
always saying and doing
crazy things that would
never occur to him.

Vive La Différence

A Mensch...

realizes that there is
a good reason for
the term "opposite sex."
She understands that
he marches to the beat
of a different drummer.

A Schlemiel...

insists that his S.O.
must be the one
with the problem
whenever his words
or actions disturb her.
"If you don't like it,
too damn bad!"

WE CAN WORK IT OUT

A Mensch...
is willing to talk it over.
She knows that it really
doesn't matter who
is "right" or "wrong."
She listens to what
her S.O. has to say,
and seeks a compromise.

A READY - MADE
PUNCHING BAG

A Schlemiel...

can't wait to take out his
frustrations on his S.O.
after a bad day.
Although she is totally
innocent, she's such
a convenient target.

MAKE LOVE, NOT WAR

A Mensch...
would never blame
her S.O. for her bad day.
Instead of greeting him
by "biting his head off,"
she asks for a big hug.

FAMILIARITY
BREEDS CONTEMPT

A Schlemiel...

can (and does) say
terrible things to
his S.O., that he would
never say to anyone else.
He uses the privacy
of his home to
verbally abuse her.

No Hitting
Below The Belt

A Mensch...

may become upset,
but does not allow
herself to descend to
the depths of depravity.
She never resorts to
the use of insults
as a weapon.

A Schlemiel...

is forever dredging up
past mistakes when
he thinks he's losing
an argument with his S.O.
"So what if I goofed?
Five years ago you
wrecked the car!"

DON'T LOOK BACK

A Mensch...

doesn't try to shift
the blame by bringing up
ghosts from the past.
She knows that nothing
will be resolved by
reminding her S.O. of
his prior transgressions.

71

BURSTING HER BUBBLE

A Schlemiel...

responds to his S.O.
with a yawn anytime
he is not impressed
with one of her ideas.
So what if she thinks
it's wonderful —
he couldn't care less.

Don't Rain
On My Parade

A Mensch...

offers encouragement
to her S.O. whenever
he is enthusiastic about
something, even if she
privately has her doubts
as to the wonder of it all.

A Schlemiel...

believes that his S.O.
should change for him.
In his mind, no sacrifice
is too great — as long as
SHE'S the one
making the sacrifice.

A Mensch...

regards her S.O. as an equal partner, believing his priorities to be just as important as her own. In any good relationship, both parties must be willing to compromise.

Do not be discouraged if your early relationships don't turn out well — they rarely do.
It is much easier to appreciate the right S.O. if you have already been with the wrong one.

SILENCE IS GOLDEN

When your S.O. makes
a minor error, let it go.
All you will accomplish
by repeatedly pointing
it out is poisoning the
atmosphere — and do
you really want to
start a war?

THINKING OF GETTING HITCHED?

If your S.O. has a close relationship with his/her family, an important factor to consider is how well you will fit in. When you tie the knot, you will be marrying the whole family!

My Bed Or Yours?

If you and your S.O. don't see eye-to-eye on the room temperature or what to watch on TV, why not consider separate bedrooms? This may even help to "rekindle the flame."

SLEEPING WITH
THE ENEMY — NOT!

Arguments and anger
are unavoidable,
especially with your S.O.
But you **must** learn to
forgive and forget ASAP.
Living with your S.O.
as a "temporary enemy"
is a no-win situation.

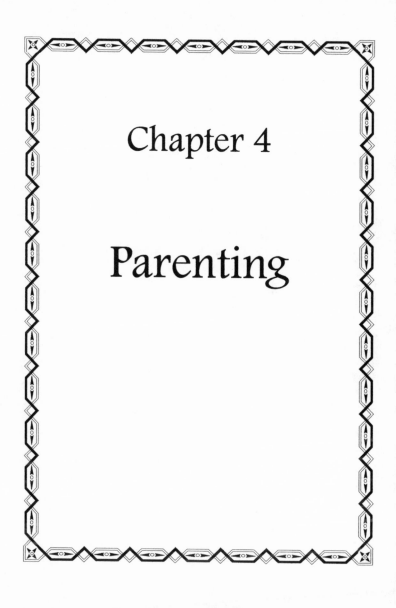

Chapter 4

Parenting

To Err Is Human

Don't be afraid to say "I'm sorry" to your kids. It's important for them to learn that everyone makes mistakes — and that absolutely no one should be too big to admit it.

LIVING VICARIOUSLY THROUGH HIS CHILDREN

A Schlemiel...

tries to erase his own athletic failures with a constant verbal barrage. Unfortunately, his bellowing from the bleachers ruins the game for everyone.

A Mensch...

realizes that her child's sporting event is HER CHILD'S sporting event. She offers encouragement without calling attention to herself.

A Schlemiel...

dreads it when it's his
turn to drive a car full
of children to the park.
Playing chauffeur to a
bunch of screaming brats
is not his idea
of a good time.

A Mensch...

enjoys her free days
when she does not
have to do the driving.
When it **is** her turn,
that's good — now she
can discover what's going
on in the neighborhood.

A Schlemiel...

is too busy with
his own concerns
to listen to his children
talk about their day.
He thinks, "Who cares
what you did at recess?
I've got things to do."

A Mensch...

pays attention when
her children want to
tell her about their day —
that's important to her.
Even a busy executive
can find 15 minutes
to spend with her kids.

A Schlemiel...

tries to recapture his
youth by "hanging out
with the gang."
He is oblivious to the fact
that his teenagers are
totally mortified
by his presence.

A Mensch...

tactfully withdraws
when her teenagers
are with their friends.
She knows the rule;
parents should be seen
and not heard — and
not seen very often.

A Schlemiel...

yells at his kids when
they make a mistake.
He's so busy jumping
all over them, he fails to
realize that all he's doing
is making them
feel even worse.

PATIENCE IS A VIRTUE

A Mensch...

doesn't fly off the
handle when her kids
do something wrong.
Instead, she patiently
explains how to do it
better next time.

REMBRANDT HAD TO START SOMEWHERE

Art is an excellent way
for children to express
their creativity.
Praise their work,
even if you have no idea
what you're looking at.
"That's beautiful honey,
look at all those colors!"

The Buck Stops Here

Your parents will tell you that it's their job to spoil the grandchildren. But if they cross the line by undermining your parental authority, you may have to remind them that **you** are now the boss.

MY DOOR IS
ALWAYS OPEN

If you want your kids
to share their problems
with you, you must
earn their confidence.
Be open and receptive;
if they feel comfortable
talking to you, chances
are they will open up.

SITTING ON THE BENCH ONLY GETS YOU SPLINTERS

Involve your children in some sort of team sport. This will improve their coordination, as well as teach them about good sportsmanship and how to interact with others.

MONEY CAN'T
BUY ME LOVE

You don't need to spend
a lot of money to
make your children happy.
While all kids love
receiving gifts, often
what they really need
is quality time with you.

UNITED WE STAND, DIVIDED WE FALL

Always present a united front to your children. They are clever and will not think twice about **running** to Dad when Mom says no. Communication between parents is the key.

Regardless of age
or gender, children need
an occasional display
of affection.
But when they get older,
they much prefer that
you hug them
when nobody's looking.

E.T. Phone Home

If you want your "adult" children to call you more often, consider getting an "800" number. It makes things easier for them, and it costs less than you might think.

MOM, I'M GETTING MY NOSE PIERCED

Expect your children
to test your resolve and
your patience, sometimes
in a shocking way.
Remain calm and don't
lose your head.
Often all they really want
is to get your attention.

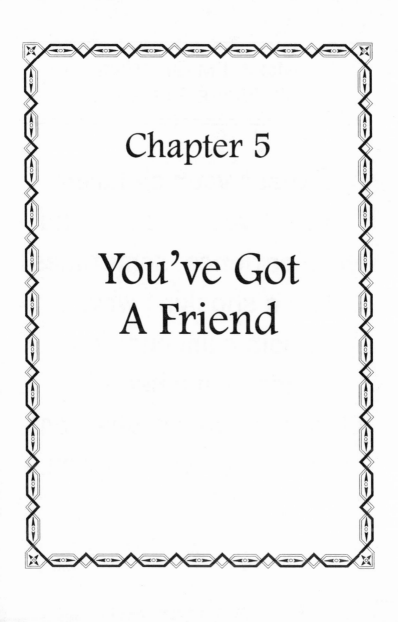

Chapter 5

You've Got A Friend

MIRROR, MIRROR
ON THE WALL

Some people look
in the mirror and see
only lines and wrinkles.
Others look in the mirror
and smile, knowing they're
looking at the best friend
they will ever have.

EAGER TO POUNCE

A Schlemiel...
is so insecure that
he never misses an
opportunity to criticize
his friends when
they screw up.
In fact, he even
looks forward to it.

A Mensch...

does not live to correct her friends, and does so only when necessary. If she needs to point out an error, she is careful to phrase it in a way that won't hurt your feelings.

A Schlemiel...

thinks he is perceptive
enough to size someone
up within five minutes.
Then he is shocked
to discover that his
new best friend is really a
wolf in sheep's clothing.

A Mensch...

avoids snap judgments,
because first impressions
can often be misleading.
She needs time to
find out what makes
a person tick before
getting close to them.

A Schlemiel...

expects your help anytime he's in trouble — but if you're in a bind, forget it! "Your car broke down and you need a ride? I can't leave now, the game just went into overtime!"

A Mensch...

is someone you can
count on — she's not just
a fair-weather friend.
She knows that
"a friend in need is
a friend indeed."

AFTER ALL I'VE DONE FOR HIM

A Schlemiel...

feels insulted if a friend
fails to return his phone
call in a timely fashion.
He may even consider
ending the friendship.
"If he's gonna be like
that, who needs him!"

A Mensch...
gives her friends
the benefit of the doubt.
She realizes that one
unreturned call isn't
the end of the world.
She's more than willing
to try again.

A Schlemiel...

gets upset when a friend
responds to his problem
by offering good advice.
"Shut up! All I want
is for you to listen
to what I'm saying!"

A Mensch...

lets you know up front whether she's looking for advice or if all she wants is a shoulder to cry on. Being her friend is easy because you always know exactly where you stand.

A Schlemiel...

tries to talk you out of
doing something if
that's not the way
he would have handled it.
He's so self-absorbed
that what **you** really want
never enters his mind.

To Each Her Own

A Mensch...

is supportive of your way
of doing things, even if
she might have done it
differently herself.
She doesn't presume
to run your life —
her own is quite enough!

Beware The Chameleon

A Schlemiel...

secretly gets a kick out of
watching a friend fail.
In fact, by delaying vital
information until it's
too late, he sets you up
so that you must go wrong.

A Mensch...

is eager for her friends
to succeed, and wouldn't
dream of holding back
useful information.
You can count on her
to be on your side.

A GOOD LISTENER IS
WORTH 10 THERAPISTS

We all need someone
we can talk to about
anything and everything.
Whether or not you're
seeking advice, a special
friend enables you to feel
comfortable discussing
whatever is on your mind.

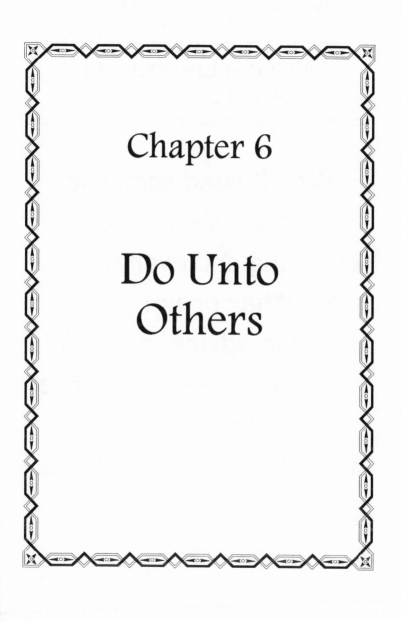

Chapter 6

Do Unto Others

He Who Hesitates Is Lost

Any phone call or e-mail
that is worth returning
should be returned
as soon as possible.
Isn't that what
you would want
if you were the person
awaiting a response?

A Schlemiel...

always has an answer,
even if he doesn't have
the slightest idea
what he's talking about.
He would never dream
of saying, "I don't know."

HONESTY IS THE BEST POLICY

A Mensch...

is never reluctant
to admit that she doesn't
have the answer.
She would never
lead you astray with
inaccurate information.

Making A Mountain Out Of A Molehill

A Schlemiel...

delights in pouncing on
people for any little error.
He builds himself up
by bringing others down.
"Only a shmo would do
something *that* stupid."

A Mensch...

doesn't need to put others down in order to make herself feel good. She is willing to overlook minor mistakes, because everyone makes them.

A Schlemiel...

can't be bothered trying
to earn the respect
of those around him —
he simply expects it.
However, his shtick
doesn't impress anyone.

R-E-S-P-E-C-T, FIND OUT
WHAT IT MEANS TO ME

A Mensch...
understands that,
in order to earn respect
you first have to give it.
She doesn't have to
put on a performance
in order to be respected.

An Insincere Yes - Man

A Schlemiel...
is always there with
a quick "yes," despite the
fact that he doesn't have
the slightest intention
of following through.
Although you're deceived,
he gets to "save face."

THINK NOW, SPEAK LATER

A Mensch...

avoids impulsive answers.
She's not afraid to say,
"Let me get back to you."
This gives her the time to
think it over carefully,
so she can provide you
with an honest answer.

In Love With The Sound Of His Own Voice

A Schlemiel...

is constantly
interrupting you.
He doesn't care about
what you're saying — why
should he hear you out?
"You don't know anything;
just stifle yourself!"

A Mensch...

is genuinely interested
in what you have to say.
She allows you to finish
your thoughts because
she knows that she can
learn more from listening
than from talking.

A Schlemiel...

rattles off his number at
the speed of light when
leaving a phone message.
Confucius says:
"If your message
isn't clear, you won't
hear back within a year."

A Mensch...

speaks slowly and clearly
when leaving her number.
She wants to make sure
her call will be returned,
not leave you struggling
to figure out the number.

A Schlemiel...

is often late, but never
thinks to call ahead.
"What's your problem?
I showed up, didn't I?"
Of course, heaven help
you if **you** show up late —
he goes absolutely nuts.

A Mensch...

knows that leaving people hanging is inconsiderate. She makes every effort to plan ahead, but if she's running late or is unavoidably detained, she will let you know.

CARNAC
THE MAGNIFICENT

A Schlemiel...

is always telling you what
you're thinking and why
you did what you did —
even though he
could not possibly know.

A Mensch...

knows better than to
act like a mind-reader.
She gives you a chance
to express your thoughts
without putting words
in your mouth.

A Very Unworthy Recipient

A Schlemiel...

doesn't bother to acknowledge a gift. He's too busy dreaming about the Playboy calendar he didn't get to take the time to send you a thank-you note.

IT IS THE THOUGHT THAT COUNTS

A Mensch...

appreciates your taking the time to pick something out for her. She always makes sure to acknowledge your thoughtfulness.

A Schlemiel...

becomes obsessed
with revenge when
his feelings are hurt.
All he can think about
is what it will take
to "even the score."

TWO WRONGS DON'T MAKE A RIGHT

A Mensch...
knows that seeking
revenge is not practical
or constructive.
Instead of devoting
her energy to cooking up
a sinister plot, she moves
on to better things.

A Schlemiel...

is always ready, willing, and able to bombard you with the "wisdom of his words," despite the fact that you didn't ask for his advice.

A Mensch...

never needs to act like
an obnoxious yenta.
She gives advice only
in two cases — either
because you asked for it,
or when a crisis demands
that she speak up.

A Schlemiel...

is fanatical about perfect table manners, and lives for the chance to pounce on unsuspecting dinner companions. "What kind of idiot eats steak with a salad fork!"

A Mensch...

believes that silverware
should not be used
to express hostility.
She would never spoil a
nice dinner by harping on
anyone for a lack of
utensil expertise.

Tell 'Em Something Good

The need for praise
does not vanish with age.
If you admire what
someone has done,
whether they are
six, thirty-six, or sixty,
let them know.

RETURNING THE FAVOR

When someone makes
your day, consider
showing your gratitude
by being very generous.
Your kind gesture will be
much appreciated —
and now you've made
someone else's day!

BEFORE A DISCUSSION BECOMES A FIGHT

Minor disagreements
need not become
World War III.
Listen carefully,
wait your turn,
and if all else fails —
agree to disagree.

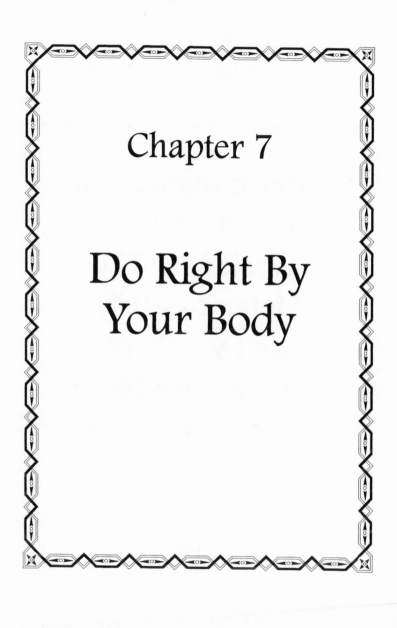

Chapter 7

Do Right By Your Body

How Much Is Enough?

Health experts
recommend that you drink
one ounce of water
for every two pounds
of body weight each day.
A 200-pound body needs
100 oz. of water.

LOW CAL MAY
EQUAL HIGH RISK

A Schlemiel...
frequently overeats,
but he proudly cuts
a few calories by using
a sugar substitute.
"Would you believe —
each packet has
only one calorie!"

A Mensch...

knows that doctors are concerned about the health risks posed by the excessive use of artificial sweeteners. She uses only healthy sugar alternatives.

Getting All Juiced Up

A Schlemiel...

thinks that drinking large quantities of fruit juice is good for his health. What he doesn't know is that he's pushing his blood sugar up and up.

THE FRUIT AND
NOTHING BUT THE FRUIT

A Mensch...
skips the juice, and eats
the whole fruit instead.
She gets extra nutrients
and fiber by
eating a natural,
unprocessed food.

Gotta Have His Cake
And Eat It Too

A Schlemiel...

eats a big dinner
and tops it off with a
lavish dessert — he can't
resist the sweets.
"It came free with the
meal — I'll just let out
my belt another notch."

SAVE ROOM
FOR THE GOODIES

A Mensch...

thinks ahead when
she orders her dinner.
If she intends to have
dessert, she makes sure
to choose a smaller meal.
She never overeats
"because it's there."

A Schlemiel...

fools himself into believing that he is invulnerable.

He refuses to see a doctor until the problem is totally out of control.

A Mensch...

realizes that "no pain"
is not the same as
"no problem."
If she doesn't feel right,
she won't hesitate to call
the doctor and have it
checked out.

A Schlemiel...

is always munching on a sweet or salty snack. "Yeah, I know this is my third bag of chips, but c'mon, they're small bags — look, this one is already empty."

A Mensch...

diverts a "snack attack"
by drinking some water.
She is aware that often,
when you think
you are hungry,
you are merely thirsty.

163

TAKING CARE
OF BUSINESS

When you have difficulty
going to the bathroom,
try sitting with your
feet up on a small stool,
keeping your knees bent.
Strange as it may sound,
it really does work.

IT'S NOT NUTS
TO EAT NUTS

Many nuts are a good
source of fiber, protein,
and other nutrients.
In addition, they contain
essential oils that
benefit the heart, brain,
and blood vessels.

CALLING ALL MEN

Raw pumpkin seeds
provide nutrients that
are beneficial to
a healthy prostate gland.
Don't think twice —
proceed immediately
to your nearest
health food store.

WHAT EVERY WOMAN
SHOULD KNOW

Recent studies indicate that you can help prevent urinary tract infections by drinking 2 ounces of cranberry juice daily. If you don't care for the taste, try mixing it with another liquid.

Floss First, Brush Second

When cleaning your teeth, always floss before brushing. Removing deposits between teeth and gums will allow your toothbrush to clean more thoroughly.

LET THE PROFESSIONAL HANDLE IT

If you have difficulty
taking care of your teeth,
arrange to see your
dentist more often.
The cost of a cleaning
is still less than
the cost of a filling.

A New Spin On PB&J

Even if you use "natural" peanut butter without added sugar, you still get a good deal of fat along with the protein. A healthy alternative is almond butter — much lower in saturated fats.

If you didn't bring your first-aid kit, don't panic. You can stop a cut from bleeding by sprinkling ground black pepper on it. This "home remedy" does sting, but will do until you can get proper treatment.

THAT'S WHY THEY CALL IT "JUNK FOOD"

If you love junk food, be prepared to deal with future health problems. Don't fool yourself into believing that your body will take the abuse of a poor diet without making you pay for it later.

BREAKFAST OF CHAMPIONS

Include a source of protein with breakfast. It supplies the energy you need to get rolling, and may help you to function more efficiently.

A Mile A Day
Keeps The Doctor Away

A recent study indicated
that regular exercise
and a proper diet may do
even more for your health
than medication.
Check with your doctor
first, and then
let the walking begin!

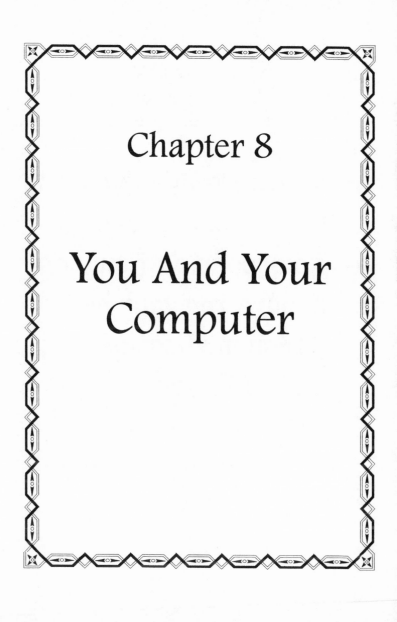

Chapter 8

You And Your Computer

CAN'T LIVE WITH 'EM, CAN'T LIVE WITHOUT 'EM

When your computer freezes or refuses to do what you want, it's perfectly natural to give dirty looks, mutter, or even swear. On the other hand, think where you'd be without it.

Better Safe Than Sorry

You can't save too often.
Don't just save to your
C-drive, but also "backup"
your files to disk or CD.
The horror stories
of people who lost hours
worth of work could
almost fill a hard drive.

Empty Your Drive
When Saying Good Night

Be sure to remove
all disks and CD's
from your computer
before you turn it off.
Otherwise, when you
turn it back on, it may
become confused.

To Me, From Me

Need a reminder?
Send yourself an e-mail.
This is also a good way
to see how your e-mail
will appear to others,
because the spacing
of the words may change
when you send it.

A Clean Machine
Is A Happy Machine

Dust, dirt, and static electricity can cause serious damage to your computer, especially the monitor and disk drives. But don't use a wet rag; use cleaning materials designed for computers.

Your printer can create power surges that may overload even the best surge protector. Always use two surge protectors; one for your computer, and one for your printer.

Two names to remember: scandisk and defrag. Running them both will prevent many headaches. If you're not sure how, or want your computer to run them automatically, ask a maven for help.

Keep The Wolves At Bay

Viruses can attack
your computer without
warning, and can cause
permanent damage.
Be sure to install and use
an anti-virus program
that will alert you
to unwanted guests.

THE BOY
WHO CRIED WOLF

Many "virus alerts"
are false alarms.
Check with one of
the following websites
before taking any action.
www.vmyths.com
www.McAfee.com
www.Norton.com

A Little Extra Protection

Make !0000 the first entry in your address book, as just a "name," with no e-mail address. By doing so, you may prevent certain viruses from spreading to all the contacts on your list.

No Peeping Toms Allowed

If you enjoy the internet, you need a good "firewall" program. Otherwise, hackers can get access to your personal data — and even make changes to it!

If You're Not
A Computer Maven

Call your local college
or high school and inquire
about a nice young person
who will come to
your home and tutor you
for a modest fee.
It will make a
world of difference.

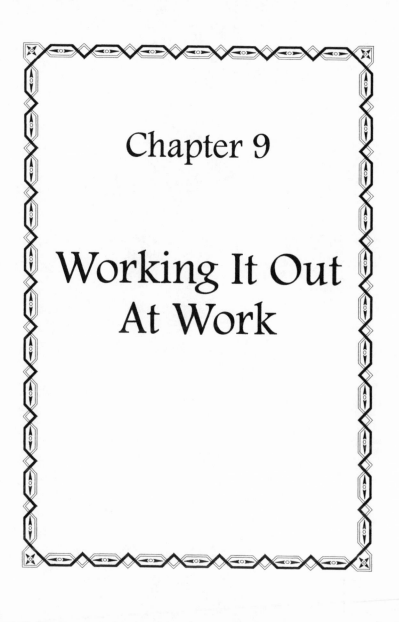

Chapter 9

Working It Out
At Work

WHO'S ON FIRST?

In any business
relationship, it's essential
to decide in advance
"who does what."
Until this is done,
you can't expect the work
to proceed smoothly.

THE EMPEROR
HAS NO CLOTHES

A Schlemiel...

prefers to surround
himself with "yes-men."
He is deathly afraid
that anyone else will
expose his shortcomings
for all the world to see.

A Mensch...

insists that the
people around her
think for themselves.
She doesn't need
to contantly be told
how wonderful she is.

A Schlemiel...

babbles incessantly,
he just never shuts up.
Although he'll talk your
ear off in the planning
stages, when it's time
to actually do something,
he's nowhere to be found.

A Mensch...

doesn't disappear when
she is most needed.
She's ready and willing
to do "whatever it takes."
You can count on her
to get the job done.

A Schlemiel...

"plants himself" at
his desk, consumed by the
need to finish his
work and go play golf.
Unfortunately, his
now-aching back won't
allow him to play at all.

A Mensch...
never sits at her desk
for too long.
Every so often, she
gets up, stretches, and
takes a deep breath.
No back problems for her.

THE BOSS
WILL NEVER KNOW

A Schlemiel...

spends most of his day
goofing off, daydreaming
about the hole-in-one
he just missed yesterday.
Of course, when the boss
walks by, he pretends
to be hard at work.

A Mensch...

takes her professional responsibilities seriously. She looks forward to relaxing at break time, but she wouldn't dream of "chasing rainbows" just because no one is looking.

IS THERE A YES - MAN IN THE HOUSE?

A Schlemiel...

asks you to comment on his work only when he's looking for praise. If you don't tell him what he wants to hear, he responds with anger and hostility.

A Mensch...

encourages her
co-workers to speak up,
and give her an honest
evaluation of her work.
As a team player, she
knows that two heads are
usually better than one.

A Schlemiel...

concentrates his efforts
on trying to figure out
who is to blame.
When he believes that
he's innocent, he can't
wait to tell the world.
"It's not my fault!"

WON'T PLAY
THE BLAME GAME

A Mensch...

has more important
things to do than waste
her time and energy
identifying "the culprit."
She's much too busy
seeking the solution
to the problem.

HASTE MAKES WASTE

A Schlemiel...

rushes to get his work over with, not caring if he does a sloppy job. When the result is a total disaster, he blows it off. "Oh well, tomorrow is another day."

ANY JOB WORTH DOING IS WORTH DOING WELL

A Mensch...

takes pride in her work. She takes as much time as she needs to get it right the first time. Tomorrow she's ready to begin her next assignment.

MACHO MAN

A Schlemiel...

assumes he can do any job he is assigned, even if it's all Greek to him. He thinks that asking for help is a sign of weakness — and blindly forges ahead.

A Mensch...

likes to know exactly
what is expected of her.
She has witnessed
too many disasters based
on incorrect assumptions
and miscommunication.

HOLD ON TO
WHAT YOU'VE GOT

If you are ever seriously tempted to quit your job, make sure that you first consider how quitting will affect your finances. Unless you have a new job lined up, be prepared to "dine" on stale bread.

Chapter 10

Vacation ~ Yes!

CONVEYOR BELTS
GET HUNGRY SOMETIMES

Make sure your
personal information
is prominently displayed
inside your luggage.
If your tags get torn off,
the airline can still
determine the owner
of the bags.

SHOULD HAVE
STAYED HOME

A Schlemiel...

shleps his worries
along with him
wherever he goes.
Because he is not able
to relax, his vacations
are as stressful as
the rest of his life.

PACK UP YOUR TROUBLES –
AND LEAVE THEM BEHIND

A Mensch...
uses vacation time
to relax and unwind.
She sees it as
an opportunity to refresh
and re-create herself,
mentally and physically.

A Schlemiel...
tries to take half
of his household goods
on vacation, so that he
can be "comfortable."
Then he kvetches about
keeping track of
so many bags.

A Mensch...

enjoys the comforts
of home, but sends
her "stuff" ahead.
What a pleasure it is
when she arrives at
her destination to find
it all waiting for her.

A Schlemiel...

rushes to see the sights after an overseas flight. "I didn't fly across the ocean to sit in my room." Before you know it, he's so tired, he's forgotten the name of his hotel.

BEFORE YOU DROP,
MAKE SURE TO STOP

A Mensch...
allows herself time to
adjust after her flight.
She understands the
effects of jet lag,
and makes sure
that her first day abroad
is a relaxing one.

ROME WASN'T BUILT IN A DAY

Select the attractions that you are most interested in, and don't feel obligated to "do it all." A seasoned traveler always prefers quality rather than quantity.

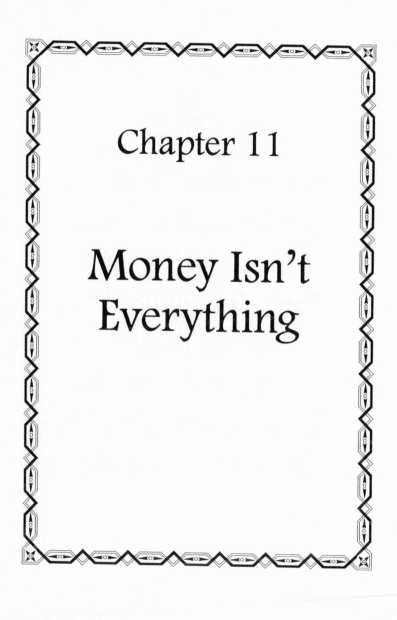

Chapter 11

Money Isn't Everything

As Long As You Don't Get Carried Away

When you're considering buying something, the most important factor should NOT be the cost. If a moderate purchase makes your life easier or brings you peace of mind, whip out that credit card!

A Schlemiel...

is a sucker for the latest
multifunction device.
"A gadget that does
everything — wow!
What a bargain!"
If only he could
get it to work!

SIMPLE TOOLS ARE
SIMPLY BETTER

A Mensch...

prefers a device that
is designed to handle
one function only.
Any product that
promises to do
too many things often
does none of them well.

KEEPING UP WITH THE JONESES

A Schlemiel...

measures his happiness
by counting his money,
tallying his possesions,
and boasting about
his romantic conquests.
Impressing others
is what he lives for.

Money Can't Buy Me Love

A Mensch...

values her relationships
with family and friends
more than material things.
She doesn't need
a mansion or a mink coat
to be happy with her life.

A Schlemiel...

has no use for
discount stores and
"bargain basements."
As for dollar stores,
you must be joking!

A Mensch...

knows that some items
sold at discount stores
are identical to the pricey
stuff sold elsewhere.
She is proud of herself
when she can avoid
throwing money away.

TREAT YOURSELF TO A
MORTGAGE - BURNING PARTY

If you are able to pay off
a mortgage or other loan,
consider doing so.
Knowing that you own
something "free and clear"
will do more for your
mental health than
saving a little on taxes.

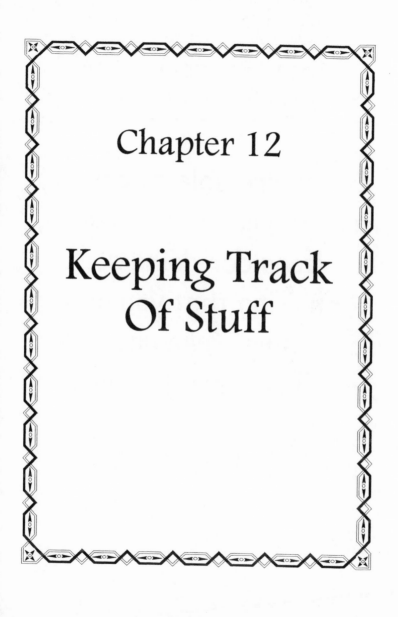

Chapter 12

Keeping Track Of Stuff

ROME WASN'T BUILT IN A DAY

Being extremely
well-organized
is admirable, yet
difficult to achieve.
But don't give up!
Even if you make only
a few improvements,
life will be a lot easier.

A Schlemiel...

believes that he can
remember all of his
worthwhile ideas without
ever writing them down.
Of course, because
he has very few,
this actually is possible.

232

THE PEN IS MIGHTIER
THAN THE SWORD

A Mensch...

knows better than to rely
on her imperfect memory.
She always keeps a
notebook and pen handy,
unwilling to lose
anything of value.

A Schlemiel...

is much better at starting projects than he is at finishing them. He can't stay focused — although he's always working, he takes forever to complete a single task.

SLOW AND STEADY
WINS THE RACE

A Mensch...
focuses on one task
at a time, and makes sure
to finish each job before
moving on to the next.
She'll never be
overwhelmed by a dozen
unfinished projects.

COVERING YOUR BUTT

Photocopy both sides of
all your credit cards
and your license.
Make sure you have the
phone numbers to call
for each one.
Keep everything in a safe,
easy-to-find place.

IN CASE YOUR WALLET
IS STOLEN

Cancel all credit cards,
and file a police report.
Call these four agencies:
Equifax 800-525-6285
Experian 888-397-3742
TransUnion 800-680-7289
Social Security fraud line
800-269-0271

LABELS – WORTH THEIR WEIGHT IN GOLD

Ever wasted an afternoon searching through boxes? Next time, use self-stick labels to summarize the contents of each box. Labeling things as you put them away will make your life much easier.

WHERE, OH WHERE HAS THAT PHONE NUMBER GONE?

When you write down something important, make sure you can find it again when you need it. A good way to do this is to keep a notebook in an easily accessible place, such as near the phone.

Want to know exactly what you did with those holiday decorations? Save yourself a headache by keeping a list of <u>where</u> things are stored, so that you can easily find what you need.

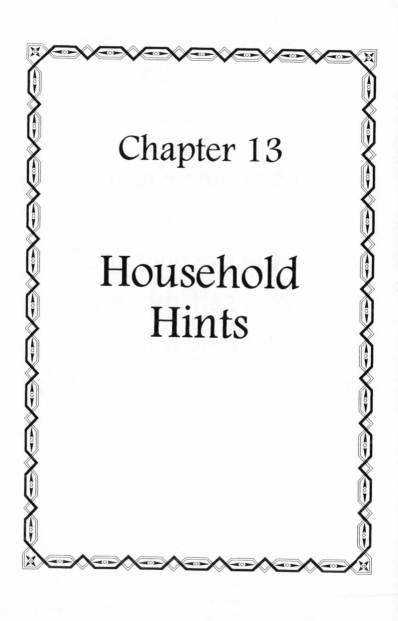

Chapter 13

Household
Hints

How Old Is That Egg?

Place the uncooked egg
in a bowl of cold water
deep enough to cover it.
If it lies flat or stands
at an angle, bon appétit.
If it stands on end,
it is questionable.
If it floats, throw it out!

BAY LEAVES – NOT JUST FOR SOUP

Many crawling insects
are repelled by
the smell of bay leaves.
If you strategically
place a few leaves
in your kitchen drawers
and cupboards, you can
keep the bugs at bay.

THE ANTS GO
MARCHING OUT

To keep ants away, place whole cloves or sage along the edges of floors, doors, and windows. Wiping your countertops with a solution of $\frac{1}{2}$ water and $\frac{1}{2}$ white vinegar will also do the trick.

An Apple A Day —
But Not A Mushy One

Apples spoil much faster
at room temperature.
If they are ripe, be sure
to refrigerate them.
They will last longer in
the fridge if you separate
them by wrapping them
in paper towels.

FRUIT FOR THOUGHT

Not sure if
that peach is ripe?
Stick a toothpick in
the fruit at the stem end.
If it goes in easily
and comes out clean,
the fruit is ripe
and ready to eat.

Non - Chemical Warfare

Rabbits detest the smell of marigolds. If you plant some all the way around your vegetable garden, you will be able to discourage unwanted bunny-munching.

THE PEPPERMINT TWIST

Mice hate the smell
of fresh peppermint.
Plant it around your house
to discourage them
from moving in.
For indoor use, oil of
peppermint on a piece
of cloth will also work.

ONCE THE BLOOM IS OFF THE ROSE

To remove residue from flower vases, try using a solution of one tablespoon salt and one cup white vinegar. If you still have some crud left, add a little rice and shake well.

I'VE GOT THAT
SINKING FEELING

To unclog a drain, try
using a cup of salt mixed
with a cup of baking soda.
Pour the dry mix into
the drain, followed by
a pot of boiling water.

BEFORE GOOD NAIL POLISH GOES BAD

You can add weeks
to the shelf life of your
nail polish by keeping it
in the refrigerator.
Storing it cold will also
make it easier to apply.

STUCK ON YOU

When postage stamps
have gotten stuck
together, put them
in the freezer for
about ten minutes.
They'll come apart easily,
without any damage.

Don't Tread On Me

Are your tires going bald?
Insert a penny into the
grooves of the tire,
with Lincoln's head
going in first.
If the tread does not
reach the top of Abe's
head, replace the tire.

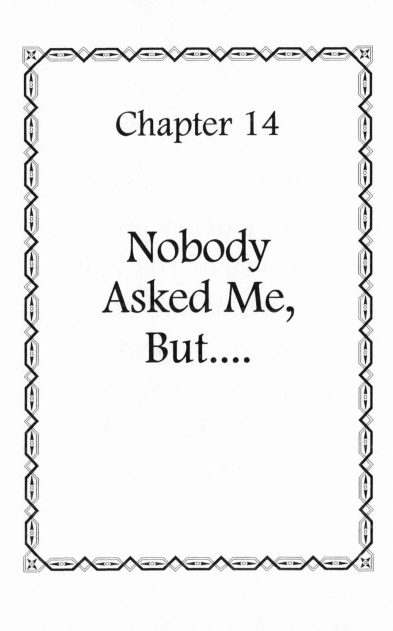

Chapter 14

Nobody Asked Me, But....

A Class Act

As long as you try to
conduct yourself with
dignity and class,
you are sure to be
admired and respected
by others who share
the same qualities.

B.S. Makes The World Go Around

A Schlemiel...

makes up excuses for the sole purpose of "covering his tush." Unfortunately, the only people he fools are other schlemiels.

A Mensch...

does not bother wasting
her time and energy
thinking up ways
to cover up mistakes.
When she is wrong,
she will freely admit it.

A Schlemiel...

loves to be a big
fish in a small pond —
the "big kahuna."
He is most comfortable
when surrounded by
shmendricks
and schlimazels.

A Distinguished Entourage

A Mensch...

knows that a smart person
surrounds herself
with smarter people.
She prefers the
company of mavens
and other mensches.

A Schlemiel...

stays in a bad relationship long after any good feelings for the other person have disappeared. "If we split up, who keeps the electric can opener?"

A Mensch...

knows that sometimes
she needs to move on.
She can be proud
of herself for having
the courage to get away
from a bad situation.

REAL MEN DON'T ASK
FOR DIRECTIONS

A Schlemiel...
would rather give up
sex than admit
that he's lost his way.
"I have no idea
where we are,
but I'm sure we're close."

A Mensch...

is not afraid to admit
she can't find her way.
She's perfectly willing
to ask a native for
directions; after all,
he might turn out
to be Brad Pitt.

265

HE CAN'T HANDLE
THE TRUTH

A Schlemiel...

is perfectly willing to
be ruled by uncertainty.
Rather than risk being
disappointed, he shies
away from finding out
what's really going on —
until it's too late.

THE TRUTH, AND
NOTHING BUT THE TRUTH

A Mensch...

is not interested in
playing "guessing games."
Whether the news
is good or bad,
she always wants
to know what's going on.

BEAUTY IS IN THE EYE OF THE RECIPIENT

When choosing a gift
for someone you cherish,
forget about what
you would like to receive.
All that matters is
what is special or
important to them.

TWO OUT OF THREE AIN'T BAD

When shopping, strive for good quality, availability, and a reasonable price. You would like to get at least two out of three; if you are ever lucky enough to get all three at once, mazel tov!

WHY RE-INVENT
THE WHEEL?

If you want to learn how
to do something, ask
someone who has already
"been there, done that."
There is nothing wrong
with benefiting from
someone else's
first-hand experience.

No one could ever
convince me to go
bungee-jumping.
However, if you apply
common sense and
a dash of moderation,
most things are worth
trying — at least once.

WHAT REAL MEN REALLY WANT

Given a choice between
a woman who has
expressed interest in him
and a more attractive one
who has not, any man
worth knowing
is more likely to pursue
the interested party.

Are you worried about how your "better half" will see you as time goes by? If so, why not consider an archaeologist as a mate? After all, who else will find you more interesting as you get older?

Don't Burn Your Bridges

Think twice before
you overreact and
"break it off" with
someone you know.
Once the relationship
has been terminated,
you may regret having
made an enemy for life.

Have you ever had
the impression that
absolutely no one cares
what you are doing,
until you are doing
something that you hope
no one finds out about?

BETTER THAN THE "DO NOT DISTURB" SIGN

While staying in a hotel, make sure to turn the TV on good and loud (unless it's late at night) when you leave the room. Thieves are less likely to enter a room if they believe that it's occupied.

KEEP YOUR FOOT
OUT OF YOUR MOUTH

Never say anything
to even remotely suggest
that you think a woman is
pregnant — until you see
an actual baby emerging
from her at that moment.

SPREAD A LITTLE CHEER TODAY

Would you like to feel better about yourself? It's really not difficult. Just find a way to make someone else feel better about themselves. That's all there is to it!

For information on
Spector Consulting Services
for Drug Discovery, Drug Development,
and Medical Writing
visit Tom's website:

http://spectors.home.mindspring.com

To learn more about yoga and meditation
classes and retreats,
visit Tom and Jo-Anna's website:

http://www.hathahouse.com

VERMONT BRIDGEFEST
with Marty Bergen

Lovely hotel in a beautiful setting
in the Green Mountains of Vermont.

Daily lectures, Q&A, and plenty of
duplicate bridge!
Special private classes also available

August 11-15, 2002

For more information contact:
Dawson's Bridge Vacations
1-800-942-6119

For Reservations call
1-800-451-6108

Hardcover Bridge Books
by Marty Bergen

Marty Sez (2001)

POINTS SCHMOINTS!
(1996 Book of the Year)

More POINTS SCHMOINTS! (1999)

Personalized autographs
available upon request

FREE shipping in the USA
when you order one or more
hardcover books!

Softcover Bridge Books
by Marty Bergen

Introduction to Negative Doubles
Better Bidding with Bergen, Vol. 1
Better Bidding with Bergen, Vol. 2
Marty's Reference Book on Conventions
Negative Doubles

For more information or to order
by credit card (all cards welcome):
1-800-386-7432

You can also contact Marty
by e-mail:
mbergen@mindspring.com